DISCOVERING MAPS

World Maps

Harriet Brundle
and John Willis

AV2
www.openlightbox.com

AV2

Step 1
Go to **www.openlightbox.com**

Step 2
Enter this unique code
UAMJPDEJU

Step 3
Explore your interactive eBook!

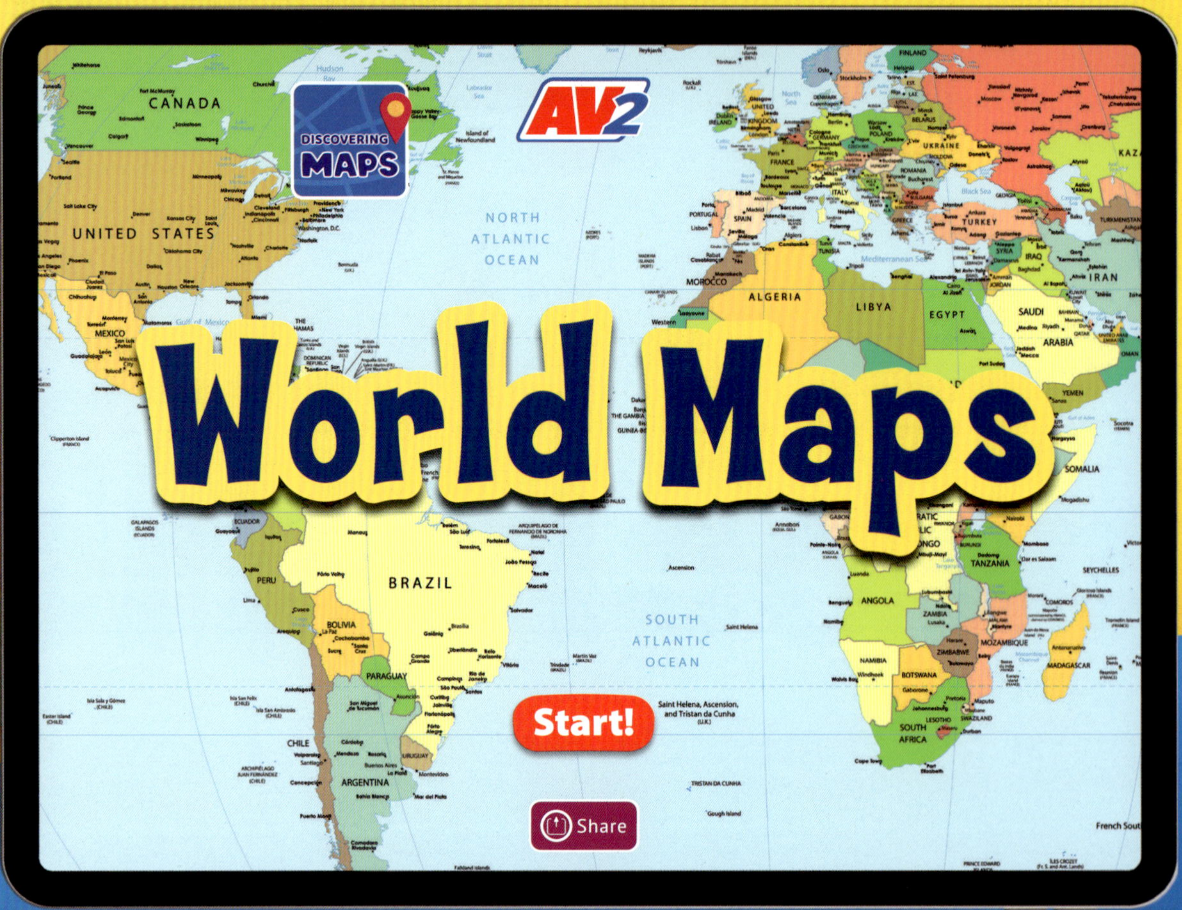

AV2 is optimized for use on any device

Your interactive eBook comes with...

- **Audio** – Listen to the entire book read aloud
- **Videos** – Watch informative video clips
- **Weblinks** – Gain additional information for research
- **Try This!** – Complete activities and hands-on experiments
- **Key Words** – Study vocabulary, and complete a matching word activity
- **Quizzes** – Test your knowledge
- **Slideshows** – View images and captions
- **Share** – Share titles within your Learning Management System (LMS) or Library Circulation System
- **Citation** – Create bibliographical references following APA, CMOS, and MLA styles

This title is part of our AV2 digital subscription

1-Year K–5 Subscription
ISBN 978-1-7911-3320-7

Access hundreds of AV2 titles with our digital subscription.
Sign up for a FREE trial at **www.openlightbox.com/trial**

The digital components of this book are guaranteed to stay active for at least five years from the date of publication.

World Maps

CONTENTS

What Is a Map?

A map is a picture that gives information about an area. Maps can show many different things, such as roads, population, or weather.

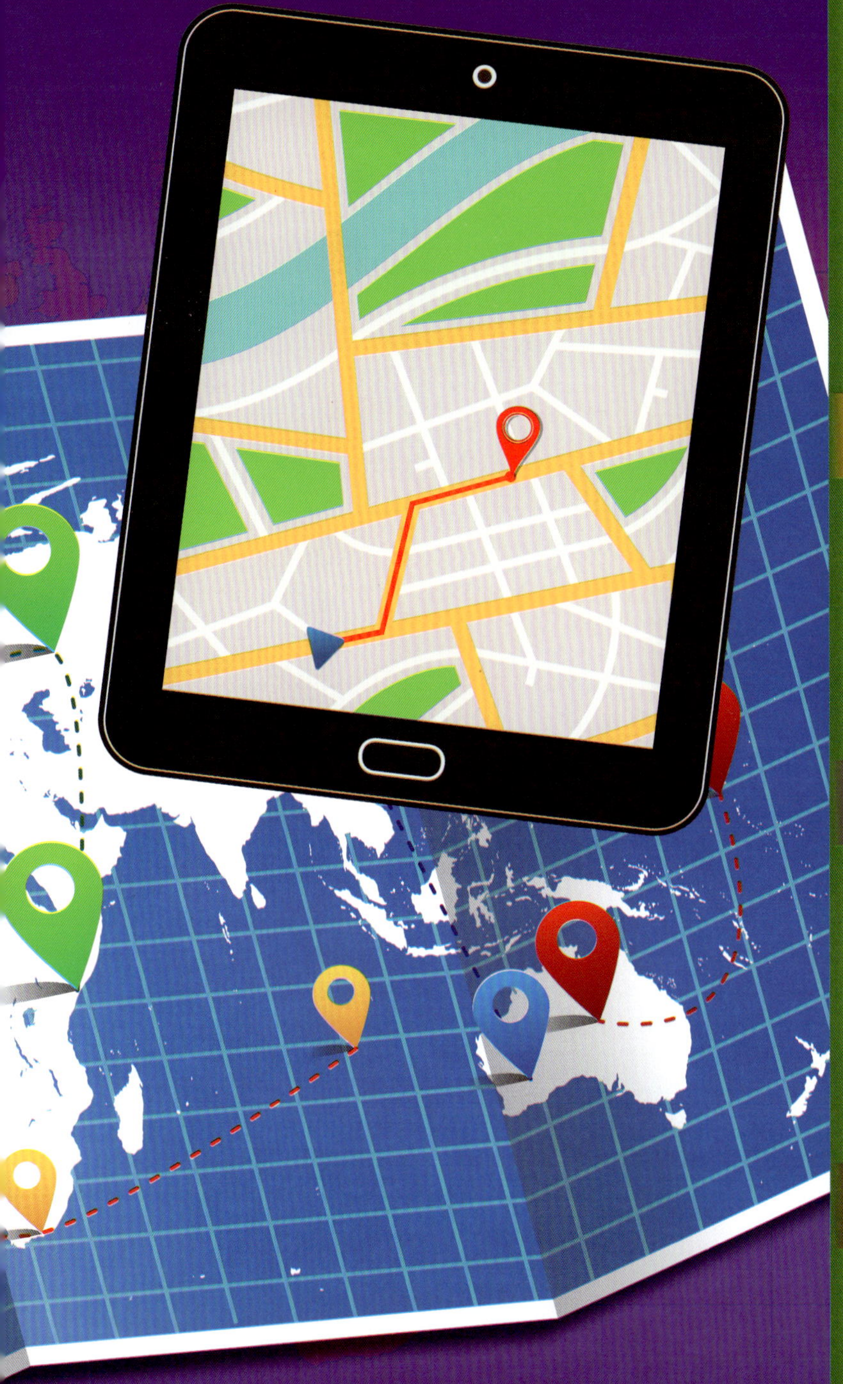

Types of Maps

Political Map

Shows country and state borders. May include major cities as well.

Physical Map

Shows geographical features. Uses shading to show how high above sea level land is.

Time Zone Map

Shows the different time zones used by countries around the world to set their clocks.

Using a Map

Maps have different colors or symbols. They represent places, countries, and landmarks.

A map key may show which color represents each continent.

Asia is the largest continent on Earth.

Map Key

You can use a map key to check what a map's symbols or colors mean.

Africa

Antarctica

Asia

Australia

Europe

North America

South America

Most maps are drawn from a "bird's-eye view." This means that they show how an area looks from above.

Each map usually has a compass printed on it. The compass shows which way on the map is north, south, east, or west.

Scale

Everything on a map has been made smaller. The amount by which things have been made smaller is called the scale.

A scale means people can show a long distance on a small map. If someone wants to know the distance across a group of countries, they can use the map scale.

World Maps

A world map is a map that shows Earth's surface.

Many world maps show all the countries in the world.

World maps also show the different oceans.

The five oceans are the Pacific, Atlantic, Indian, Arctic, and Antarctic Oceans.

Why Use a World Map?

People can use a map of the world to find out which continents are near each other.

If people would like to go to a different country, they can use a world map to find where it is.

How Is a World Map Made?

To make a map of the world, start by drawing the outlines of the larger areas of land.

Then, add the different countries that make up each continent.

There are five oceans to be added, too.

Mapping My Planet

PICK A STARTING POINT

Using a world map, start by drawing the country where you live. Then, draw the other countries around it.

ADD OTHER COUNTRIES

Next, add as many other countries as you can. Add labels to show which country is which.

ADD THE OCEANS

Add the oceans all around the countries you have drawn.

MAKE A KEY

Draw symbols for cities, forests, and other landmarks on the map to create a map key.

TOWN

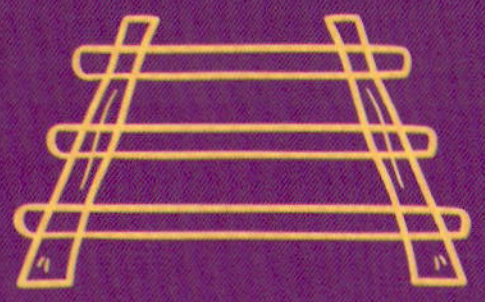

TRAIN TRACKS

FARM

CITY

LANDMARK

FOREST

OCEAN

MOUNTAINS

DESERT

Be Creative!

This is a map of the world. The borders of some countries have been marked with dotted lines.

Using another map of the world, can you work out which country is which on this map?

KEY WORDS

Research has shown that as much as 65 percent of all written material published in English is made up of 300 words. These 300 words cannot be taught using pictures or learned by sounding them out. They must be recognized by sight. This book contains 91 common sight words to help young readers improve their reading fluency and comprehension. This book also teaches young readers several important content words, such as proper nouns.

Page	Sight Words First Appearance
4	a, about, an, as, can, different, gives, is, many, or, picture, show, such, that, things, what
5	above, and, around, by, country, high, how, land, may, of, sea, set, state, the, their, to, uses, well, world
6	each, Earth, have, on, places, they, which
7	America, mean, you
8	are, eye, from, looks, most, this
9	has, it, way
10	been, made, miles
11	group, if, know, long, people, small, wants
12	all, also, in
14	find, near, other, out, why
15	go, like, where, would
16	add, be, make, start, then, there, too, up
18	live, my, point
19	next
21	city, farm, for

Page	Content Words First Appearance
4	area, information, map, population, roads, weather
5	borders, clocks, features, sea level, shading, time zones
6	Asia, colors, continent, key, landmarks, symbols
7	Africa, Antarctica, Australia, Europe, North America, South America
8	view
9	compass
10	kilometers, scale
11	distance
12	oceans, surface
13	Antarctic, Arctic, Atlantic, Indian, Pacific
16	outlines
18	planet
19	labels
21	desert, forests, town, tracks

Published by Lightbox Learning Inc.
276 5th Avenue, Suite 704 #917
New York, NY 10001
Website: www.openlightbox.com

Library of Congress Control Number available upon request.

ISBN 978-1-5105-6350-6 (hardcover)
ISBN 979-8-8745-1505-8 (softcover)
ISBN 978-1-5105-6351-3 (static multi-user eBook)
ISBN 978-1-5105-8144-9 (interactive multi-user eBook)

Printed in Guangzhou, China
1 2 3 4 5 6 7 8 9 0 28 27 26 25 24

052024
100923

Project Coordinator: John Willis
Designer: Jean Faye Rodriguez

Every reasonable effort has been made to trace ownership and to obtain permission to reprint copyright material. The publisher would be pleased to have any errors or omissions brought to its attention so that they may be corrected in subsequent printings.

The publisher acknowledges Getty Images and Shutterstock as the primary image suppliers for this title.

First published by BookLife in 2018